Thoughts &Rhymes on Modern Times

Reflections on modern-day life from the perspective
of a 90-something dinosaur

Thoughts &Rhymes on Modern Times

by Fran

BROWN
DOG
BOOKS

Published under licence by Brown Dog Books and
The Self-Publishing Partnership Ltd, 10b Greenway Farm, Bath Rd, Wick, nr. Bath BS30 5RL

www.selfpublishingpartnership.co.uk

ISBN printed book: 978-1-83952-552-0
ISBN e-book: 978-1-83952-553-7

Cover design by Andrew Prescott
Internal design by Andrew Easton

Cover and internal illustrations by Susie Robertson
FB: SusieRobertsonArt
Insta: susierobertsonart
www.susierobertsonart.co.uk
www.susierobertsonart.com
susiejrobertson@outlook.com

Printed and bound in the UK

This book is printed on FSC® certified paper

If you would like to know more about Fran, and read her new poems, why not visit her websites:
www.rhymesonmoderntimes.co.uk
and
www.rhymesbyfran.co.uk

I dedicate this book to a small band of friends
who have kept me focused and not listened to any excuses.
They know who they are.

Contents

NEW PURSUITS

When at last I finally admit
I can no longer walk, or even sit,
without some help, I am forced to see
what the rest of my life is going to be.
"Try new pursuits," others have said,
"things to explore inside your head."
"Read books, do puzzles, and soon you'll find
you won't hanker after what's left behind –
a life of sport, and adventures too!"
So I rack my brains – "what can I do?"
Words have always appealed to me,
so I'll write some down:
I'm curious to see
if they can be
a new pursuit.

A HOPEFUL DISPLAY

Now that I'm aged, I've decided to start
and grow some spuds, and flowers in carts.
It's the very first time, I'm ashamed to say,
agriculture has come to play
a part in my life.
Daily, bins and baskets arrive
but no instructions as to how they can thrive
on my little patio out the back.
I'll ring a friend who's got green fingers:
her voice in my head just lingers and lingers.
"You'll need compost and earth and fertiliser;
a small trowel and fork, and don't forget gloves!"
I'm filled with alarm and none the wiser.
So, I'll send this clobber round to my friend,
then in my mind I can see the end –
baskets of flowers of wonderful hue
and sharing with me a spud or two.
Alas I'm not the type to wear a green welly –
I'll have to go back to watching the telly!

MY EASTER BONNET

Oh how I long for an Easter bonnet
with all the flowers and do-dahs on it,
and pretty things to wear all day
celebrating a national holiday.
It's been a difficult year for all,
plenty of things we don't want to recall.
But Easter's a time to look forward, not back –
so don't ponder on it,
just wear your virtual
Easter bonnet!

THE BANK WITH NO CASH

I went to the bank to ask for some cash
in order to replenish the stash
I'd given away in dribs and drabs
over the years.

"I'm sorry Madam," the young man said,
"there's no more cash, but this, instead
you pay by cards, and online clicks –
but watch out for all the clever Dicks
who'll try to scam you!"

"Oh well," I thought, "that's quite a shock."
So now I'm going to go from here
and buy a pint
from the pub with no beer.

PERENNIAL

A vase of tulips I can see
placed on the table in front of me,
packed with tightly furled up colour.
I watch each day as the petals unfurl
and then inevitably fall
into a fading mess of colour.
But is their life finished,
their value diminished?
No, for in my heart
they'll always be an integral part
of the beauty of nature.

THE FORECAST

I patiently wait 'til the end of the news
to hear the Met Office's infallible views
on tomorrow's weather.
Always presented by cheerful folk
armed with a cane with which to poke
at various points of the whole UK.
Forecasting wind, rain, hail or snow
or even some sun, but where I don't know.
Is that a patch of blue right over my house?
All I need to know
without a doubt
is if I can hang my washing out!

ALLOTMENTS

Allotments are very hard to obtain,
the Council only grants them now and again
so some can cultivate flowers and veg,
or a little garden with a privacy hedge.
Others are envious of this way of life,
and see it as a way to alleviate strife.
But we are all unaware that at the moment of birth
every soul is allocated an allotment on earth.
As we grow older, we can fill it at will
with the fruits of our labours,
whether good or ill.
We can grow beautiful flowers of every hue,
or seed it with weeds, as some folk do.
Enrich our lives with vibrant thoughts and deeds,
and decide in the end if they meet the world's needs.

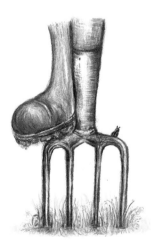

AN AROMA

The smell of toast…
what memories does it evoke for me?
Rushing to school, always late,
gobbling a buttered slice in hand,
which must be finished before the gate.
A consoling snack made by Mum,
with lots of the weirdest toppings on
when things went wrong.
Slices piled high by the side of the screen
whilst studying hard, so they won't be seen
as a sign of lazy malnourishment!
The smell of toast has remained with me –
a comforting sign of life's constancy.

HOPE

If I could persuade the sun to shine
on everyone's life
not just mine,
would it lighten the load
our world seems to share?
Relieve the fear that permeates all
and restore that sense of love and care
that maybe we're struggling to recall?
I believe myself the sun will persist
and heal us of thoughts that might resist
this beautiful outcome.

A HARD-WON PRIZE

Trophies and badges I've won in my life,
all the results of sporting strife
of one kind or another.
But where they are now I cannot say:
lost in the midst of house moves, I think,
left behind with the kitchen sink.
But now I've gone in for another prize –
much harder to win than in any sport –
just answering questions of random size
on my health and lifestyle and whether I ought
in fact to be entering for this prize.
But now in their wisdom (and receipt of ten quid)
the Council have awarded me
A BLUE BADGE!
Park where I like (almost) and usually free.
What wouldn't I give to currently be
my own driver, and whizz around and park
where I like,
but alas I'm always the passenger now,
and my drivers don't see it like me!

PAYBACK

We're all going to the seaside:
car's all loaded and ready to go.
Children not as excited as usual, it seems –
but why, I really don't know. We're off!
Stop the car! No hullaballoo!
Just help me out – I need the loo!
Are we nearly there?
Soon be time, I need some eats –
and you can't fob me off with a bag of sweets!
Don't turn round and give me that look –
I need much more than this colouring book
to keep me happy!
Why aren't we there yet?
If your dad were driving, we would be, I bet!
"Can't you drive faster?" I impatiently shout,
"by the time we arrive, the tide will be out!"
I've got castles to dig, ice creams to eat
oh boy, oh boy, revenge is so sweet
when it's part of my 90th birthday treat!

FRIENDSHIP

We go for a walk, old Betsy and I,
under the blue of the high summer sky.
She sniffs at the smells, with no reaction
to the ones that once would galvanize action
to chases and hunts and fun galore.
I know she wishes that just once more
she could jump and run
but alas that door has closed for her.
As it will for me.
I must fondly remember what used to be.
There's a decision to be made,
and soon, I see.
But please, darling Betsy –
don't leave it to me.

THE LADIES' FINAL

The players emerge from the famous tunnel,
and I must decide whose energies I'll funnel
into me.
I gaze at their outfits, the skirts so short
(would never have been allowed in my day on court!)
The warm-up has started, and now I can see
which of these ladies I'll choose to be.
The game has begun, but I'm perplexed –
I can't guess where to run to next!
The balls fly hither and thither at speed
until I reluctantly have to concede
I could never have played like this!
Still, a Pimm's, strawberries and cream,
enjoyed here on my couch,
make up for the fact
I'm just an old slouch!

HOW COME?

Fleet of foot I follow
the pristine path
that takes me through
an enchanted wood.
Everything here is smiling at me –
all the animals as cute as can be.
Trees I've never seen before
bending and whispering – they speak to my core.
As I move on now it occurs to me
I have not coughed, or been in pain;
my legs are working as they used to again.
How come?
The path leads out of this enchanted wood,
and there in the light a figure is stood:
it's like Joseph and his technicolour dreamcoat!
I'm filled with a warmth I cannot explain.
"Welcome home, my dear," the figure said,
"you have been here before, again and again."
"How come?"
I say, shaking my head,
but it's dawning on me –
my soul is alive,
my body is dead.

A REBELLION

Every morning when I awake
I must decide which form to take:
it's my ambition to be known
as completely *woke*.
So I could be gender neutral today,
wear some apparel any old way.
My clothes suit either, a formless jumble
with clodhopper boots that make me feel humble
I don't have to wear anything that fits.
When I have an urge, that's easy too
just look for a gender-neutral loo!
My family don't like this very new me,
don't want a Grandma as woke as can be,
don't like my opinions that simply don't fit
their own views on life, not even a bit.
However, with a twinkle, and to reassure them I say,
"I still shuffle round Waitrose
at the end of the day!"

AN OPENING

Everything is sealed
in impenetrable plastic.
My wrists and fingers simply can't cope,
so I'm forced to find
something more drastic.
Knives, hammers, scissors –
I try in vain
to reach the contents:
Oh no! Not again!
My blood is bright red –
that's reassuring to me,
but will they see it like this
when I visit once more
that nice A & E?

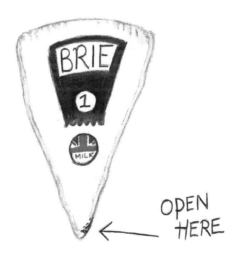

(CRUISING) – DRESSING FOR DINNER

People pacing up and down
not so different from living in a town.
A miscellany of clothes, shapes and sizes,
not competing for there are no prizes.
For comfort wear during the day
but come the evening, what can I say?
The finery's out, all smart and glitter,
even the men are trying to hit a
more suitable evening mode
to please their ladies.
But formal nights are a different scene.
You can tell where all the ladies have been –
primping and painting in salon and spa –
they carefully saved what they actually are:
ladies of leisure!
Partner forced into formal DJs
("Oh dear", he thinks,
"I might have been thinner
when I last wore this
at the Rotary dinner
two years ago!")
You can see what they think of this shipboard craze
for dressing up! Still,
everyone goes home, and talks online
about how they've had a wonderful time
and now, of course, can't wait until
they've booked themselves another thrill!

JUST PASSING

I sit and watch the clouds pass by,
chasing themselves across the sky:
sometimes in shapes I can decipher,
but mostly in formless drifts I have no eye for
discerning their meaning.
Perhaps this is how it's meant to be:
we coast along on an even keel
'til the dark clouds intrude –
that's probably the deal.

CHOICE

Isn't it enough,
oh fanciful child,
that others can survive
whilst in the wild?
Searching and seeking every day
for the means to live and find a way.
Creatures on whom we can only ponder
upon their reasons to exist.
They live to complete a cycle of life,
which seems to us to be nothing but strife.
How lucky are we, in our human way,
to have a choice in what we may
do with our lives!

A LESSON

I remember when, at the age of eight,
we played in our street from morning 'til late.
Hopscotch, skipping, blind man's buff –
we could never have enough
of these games and noise:
just a gang of girls and boys.
The mother of one was a mother to all,
so we felt quite safe, whate'er should befall.
But there was one house we never went near,
where lived a man so tall and austere.
Never spoke, never smiled so that's because
we convinced ourselves, he was the
WIZARD OF OZ!

One day when running home quite late,
I tripped at the gate
of this old man we'd decided to hate.
I howled with fright, with fear and pain,
sure I'd never see home again:
my lovely Mum – and even my brothers –
were lost to me, for ever!
The front door opened, and there he stood,
this scary old wizard, the fear of our neighbourhood!
"Well, young lady, what have we here?
Not so bad that I can see.
A bit of blood and a badly grazed knee.
Just sit on the wall, we'll clean it up,
put on a bandage, then home you hop,
your Mum will be waiting with nice things for tea."
So the lesson I learned that's stayed with me is
"NEVER JUDGE A BOOK BY ITS COVER" –
just wait and see!

MEDICATION

All my life I've been buying pills,
mostly (I think) for imaginary ills.
Over the counter, from chemists and stores
or health food shops, with never a pause
to consider either their need or effect.
Then one day, common sense kicked in:
all pills and potions consigned to the bin.
The years rushed by – as they always do –
with family, friends, some sadness too,
until I arrived at an unfortunate stage
when I really <u>do</u> need pills
because of my age.
It's very galling you see, the state that I'm in
means I can't consign them all to the bin!

A TAIL'S TALE

Owing to a chance of fate
I'm almost blind and labelled "disabled".
And when I'm inclined this fate to bewail,
I'm always chastised by the thump of a tail,
as she sits by my side, as much as to say,
"You've always got me to brighten your day.
Just think of the things you can do with me
to make your life good!
We manage the streets and traffic with care,
there is no danger when I am there!
People stop to talk and ask about me
(though must not touch as I'm working, you see).
But safely at home, and totally alone,
I can play with my toys or gnaw at a bone.
Whatever I choose to chill and relax,
one thing is certain –
I'll never fail
to give you a loving thump with my tail!"

ANGST

If I need to park my car,
I know where all the car parks are
in my vicinity.
For a small fee I can wander off
and do my own thing.
But where can I park my thoughts today,
in the same convenient, low-cost way?
I would like to leave them along with my car,
and meet a friend for a drink at a bar.
A few good laughs and meaningless chatter,
no-one to ask me, "what's the matter?"
For to tell the truth I can't explain,
and I've said to myself again and again,
"Don't worry about things you can't control –
the world will get itself out of this hole."

LIFE OF A TREE

For every tree which nature fells
and lies supine in woods and dells,
another life itself pursues.
There's food and shelter for many a creature
which our senses can only marvel at.
So need I perceive the felling of my tree
to be the end of my life as I've known it,
or may some components of me
live on to benefit others?

HOW DID I DO?

I saw a child on a lead today,
hopping and skipping and keen to play
her captor, grandma, a merry dance.
Pushing her boundaries, as children will,
secure in the certainty that nothing ill
could happen.
But as we grow into the maelstrom of life,
there is no tangible lead to guide us:
only our instincts to show us the way
and, rightly or wrongly, at the end of the day,
we can only hope that we can say,
"I tried".

GIVEN GIFTS

What if you were to be wiped out today?
"It wouldn't be fair," I hear you say.
But it's fallen into a sorry mess
and anything I create couldn't be less
than chaos.
But those of you who hear me well
must cling to your certainty and continue to tell
all who will listen – and those who will not –
that the gift you've been given
cannot be taken lightly.

THE OAPs' TREAT

I'm bored with afternoon TV,
it doesn't do a thing for me.
I know what I will do, I say –
go to the Wednesday matinee!
Ticket £2 – that's very cheap,
and one may sit in any seat!
Includes a biscuit and a cup of tea:
better not – I'd have to pee.
No gentleman invites me though
to sit with him in the back row,
so sadly down the front I troop –
because it's got a hearing loop!
A "Bright Young Thing" comes onto stage.
"This latest film is all the rage,
but first a ticket you must take
to win the raffle – a packet of cake."
When all the excitement has died down
Bright Young Thing says with a frown,
"there's something that you ought to know:
this really is an X-rated show."

Why does she need to make this clear?
We've been around for many a year,
there can't be much we haven't seen
that they could put upon a screen.
The lighting dims, the film begins.
Loads of action, lots of noise –
which are girls and which are boys?
Oh good heavens, what are they doing?
Is it what is now called "screwing"?
I can sense the audience getting tenser –
how did this get past the Censor?
When at last the end does come,
we shuffle out into the sun.
"It's scandalous, that's what I say,
we didn't do that in my day."
All agree, but never mind,
next week's film is a different kind.
We all disperse, toddle home at last,
off to use our free bus pass.

PROGRESS?

I sit in the middle of a new shopping mall,
surrounded by noise, shops and lights.
An endless rush of people going round –
small children, prams and even bikes
ridden by youngsters without a sound
except a whooshing noise.
This mayhem is progress (or so I'm told!)
and I realise it's only because I'm old
that my thoughts harken back to the time
when I lived in this town.
I focus my memories on the High Street then,
small shops in the hands of ladies or men
who knew your name, and wanted to chat
about the weather, or this and that.
There's none of them left in this town
that I loved.
I'M SAD!

OPTIMISM

The trees are bare at this time of year,
but no less beautiful for that.
The intricate twinings of trunk and branches
in a way that defies even the most talented
of human artists to portray.
Perhaps we oldies are a bit like that:
stripped of leaves, but still going strong
in our hearts and inner core.
Knowing we'll never have leaves again
shouldn't cause us too much pain.
We've all experienced a life right here
and done what we could.
There are many young saplings
in the wood.

A COMMON NEED

A malady of bums and tums
unites us all wherever it comes.
Regardless of race, dogma or creed
it reveals to us a common need
to be restored to health.
So whoever we pray to, and ask for this
it matters not.
What <u>does</u> matter though is, we cease to fight
and harm each other,
but see the light that shines upon this planet of ours
and pray that it lasts for ever.

THE SOUND OF JOY

As I sit in the garden my hopes and worries
crystallise now into sharp little flurries
that alternate between hope and despair.
But something's intruding upon my thoughts –
a sound I simply can't ignore.
I'm sure I've never heard it before
at this volume.
It comes from a tree just here on my left –
a melodious warbling that's totally bereft
of doubts or fears of what happens next!
He's programmed by nature to vocalise joy,
to call for a mate, to soar through the sky!
This essence of life which flows through us all
has lifted my spirits ...
just a bird call.

IN SEARCH OF BLISS

A state of bliss, some would say,
can come at the end of a wearisome day.
Free from restraint of clothes and shoes,
leisure things on and free to peruse
relaxing hobbies.
But alas, these are only transient hours,
and bliss soon disappears from this life of ours.

But how to achieve an inner bliss
that's not reliant on any of this
extraneous matter?
What is it anyway?
Is it total peace of mind,
eliminating thoughts of any kind
and pervading our bodies through and through
inducing a state we never knew existed?
Alas it's only seldom I can reach that goal
and experience the bliss restoring my soul.

WALKIES

A worn-out dog
is a wondrous thing.
Snug in its bed
like an uncoiled spring
until, sources renewed,
and ready once more
to drag me reluctantly
through the door
for yet another exhausting hike.
However –
this time I'll take my bike!

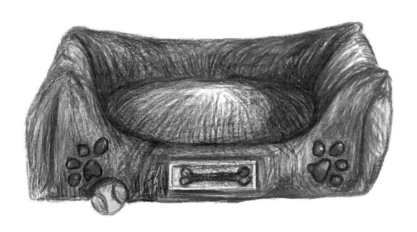

YOUR CHRISTMAS

What does Christmas mean to you?
All gifts and goodies and too much to do?
We rush to plan and wait 'til it's here,
then it's all over for another year.
But in the multicultural world today
others do not plan this way.
They have their own festivals to enjoy –
perhaps not the birth of a baby boy,
but other things for which to rejoice:
all are entitled to have a voice
in their beliefs.
So let's join together in our Christmas time
and extend our love to all of mankind.

A PRAYER FOR HEALING

We ask for your Divine help
in understanding the affliction
that rages through our planet today.
Help please all who are suffering
or bereft, and give guidance to
those brave souls striving to find
a solution.
We thank you for your everlasting
loving help, healing and support,
and may we give thanks and emerge
with more Universal love and wisdom.

UNVOICED THOUGHTS

Within these words do you think
my new pursuits could make a link
with unvoiced thoughts
of like-minded souls?
I can't decide, so I'm off to see
what two G&Ts can do for me!